Mindful thoughts for
CYCLISTS

First published in the UK and North America in 2017 by

Leaping Hare Press

An imprint of The Quarto Group
The Old Brewery, 6 Blundell Street
London N7 9BH, United Kingdom
T (0)20 7700 6700
www.QuartoKnows.com

British Library Cataloguing-in-Publication Data
A catalogue record for this book is available from the British Library

ISBN: 978-1-78240-483-5

This book was conceived, designed and produced by

Leaping Hare Press
58 West Street, Brighton BN1 2RA, UK

Publisher: *Susan Kelly*
Creative Director: *Michael Whitehead*
Editorial Director: *Tom Kitch*
Art Director: *James Lawrence*
Commissioning Editor: *Monica Perdoni*
Editor: *Jenni Davis*
Assistant Editor: *Jenny Campbell*
Designer: *Tina Smith*
Illustrator: *Lehel Kovacs*

Printed in China

10

Mindful thoughts for
CYCLISTS
Finding balance on two wheels

Nick Moore

Leaping Hare Press

Contents

A Journey of
Discovery

A family friend, sadly no longer with us, once said: 'If you want to know about something, write a book about it.'

Let me begin with a disclaimer. This is not a how-to guide, or in any way definitive on cycling or mindfulness. Nor is it a manifesto, polemic or call to arms. What it does offer, I hope, is an alternative to the slew of books that exhort us to do more, achieve more, be more. These are thoughts; reflections on finding a mindful balance in cycling – and, perhaps, in life itself. They are very much like the rides that inspired them: short, circular, with no end other than pleasure in mind.

The last decade has seen a massive resurgence in cycling's popularity in Britain and the US (it never went away in Europe) and it's a joy to see so many taking to the road for the first time, or coming back to bike-riding after what is often many years away. And in many respects, there's never been a better time to be a cyclist. The problem is that cycling, like almost everything else in life, is now highly commoditized and skilfully marketed. These thoughts are intended to help you maintain a sense of balance and proportion amid the endless temptations, illusions and distractions. As I hope they show, cycling is replete with richness, diversity, pleasure and wisdom if we are truly present, and focus on what *is*.

If you're new to cycling, I hope this book will help you cultivate a healthy, balanced relationship with your bike from the get-go. For more experienced riders, it may resonate with your own search for a new direction, or bring something extra to your regular routine. There will probably be things you disagree with, or find simply don't work for you, but my hope is that you'll find something, somewhere, in these thoughts that enables you to develop a deeper awareness as you're riding, and be fully present in the moment. It could be learning to embrace the heat, the cold, the rain. Dealing with punctures or getting lost. Noticing and appreciating the natural world. Getting up hills. Or simply being conscious of how your body and bike are working together as a single, beautiful, biomechanical entity.

I spent my thirties as a fairly typical Middle-aged Man In Lycra (MAMIL), but was forced to rethink my approach when, aged 40, I developed osteoarthritis in my knees. Suddenly, I could no longer concentrate solely on going faster and 'getting the miles in'. I had to think about every pedal stroke, be minutely aware of gradients, gearing, my position on the bike, the pressure on my knee. I had to be fully aware of everything, every moment, otherwise things started to hurt. I didn't go looking for mindfulness. It found me.

After 20 years I've started to learn what cycling truly means to me. I don't know, and would never presume to guess, what it might mean to you. That's for you, and your bicycle, to find out – mindfully – together. Enjoy the ride.

Wheels
within
Wheels

Cycling is a game played out in circles: some concentric, some interlinked like a Venn diagram. The first and smallest is described by something you can't actually see: the spindle in the bottom bracket to which the crank arms are attached. The frame is usually held to be the 'heart' of the bicycle, but in some respects, this humble metal rod is a closer analogue. Year after year, mile after mile, it works out of sight and out of mind, calmly keeping the rest of the mechanism in motion. We don't pay it any attention until it gives us trouble, and when it does, everything comes to a halt. Sometimes, it can be fixed; sometimes, the only option is to replace it. And the day will surely come when it fails altogether.

Equally vital, and similarly unsung, are the hubs. A mechanic friend of mine once told me the surest test of a hub is to put the bike in a work-stand, spin the wheel with your hand, then go and make a cup of coffee. If the wheel's still turning when you come back, it's a keeper.

ON THE SUBJECT OF PEDALLING

The next circle is concentric to the bottom bracket: the rotation of the pedals. The key to riding efficiently, in addition to correct gear selection, is a smooth, fluid pedalling action – spinning, or what the French call *la souplesse*. So important is this circle that a tired, out-of-form or just plain inept rider is said, equally vividly, to be 'pedalling squares'.

Racers aim to maintain a pedalling speed, or cadence, of about 80–90 revolutions per minute. That's about 5,000 an hour; and a typical pro will put in four to five hours a day, 200 days a year. Call it five million pedal strokes a year, over a career that might last a decade or more. Even at the more modest cadences we mortals can manage, it can soon add up over a lifetime of riding. Hence the mindful cyclist is always listening to their hips, knees and ankles: any 'twinges in the hinges' should never be ignored.

THE TURN OF THE WHEEL

Further out still, the rims and tyres are in orbit around the hubs, with the valve whizzing by like a little geostationary satellite. Laced together with their intricate tracery of spokes, they make up the whole wheel. Seamless and never-ending, containing everything and nothing, the wheel has long exerted a powerful hold on our psyche. In Buddhism, the dharmachakra has represented Gautama Buddha's teaching of the path to nirvana since ancient times. Interpretations vary, and fill whole books by themselves, but in essence, the wheel's circular shape symbolizes the perfection of the Buddha's teachings. The rim represents meditative concentration and mindfulness – it's often shown with sharp spokes protruding beyond it, signifying penetrating insights – while the hub at the centre stands for moral discipline.

In the Celtic tradition, and in modern-day paganism, the year is viewed as a wheel, revolving through the active and dormant states of nature, man and agriculture. The winter and summer solstices, and vernal and autumnal equinoxes, are marked by the solar festivals of Yule, Litha, Ostara and Mabon. Between them come the fire festivals of Imbolc, Beltane, Lughnasa and Samhain, marking significant farming events. These live on in our modern calendar as Candlemas, May Day, Lammas and All Hallows' Eve, or Hallowe'en.

THE BIG LOOP

On a road bike, every turn of the wheels takes you a about seven feet (a little over two metres); call it 750 revolutions per mile. Think how many hoops we bowl through the air, even when we just pop down to the shops. And each of these little circles described by the bicycle itself are encompassed within larger ones.

Because every ride is, ultimately, circular. Even the mightiest of them all, the Tour de France, is colloquially referred to simply as *la grande boucle* – 'the big loop'. To make these circles right through the year is to see, feel and connect with the slow roll of the seasons. There's nothing wrong with confining your cycling to warm summer days, but for true understanding we must know cold, not just heat, and embrace the dark as well as the light.

The very act of tracing these circles can help keep us intimately connected to the present moment. Only a fraction of the wheel, a few square millimetres of rubber tyre, is in contact with the ground at any given time. If that tiny patch of Earth is free of thorns, nails, spilled oil or other hazards, we remain upright, moving, and all is well. In that pure state of living entirely in the here and now, all other things forgotten, we can enjoy the full freedom, magic and sense of possibility the bicycle bestows.

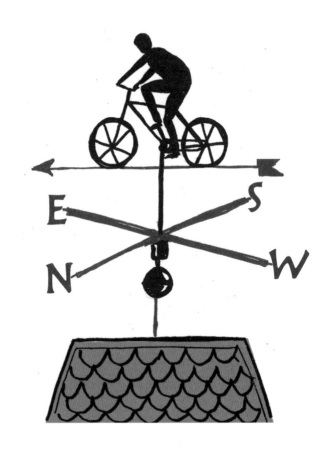

The
Wind

The ancient Greeks believed that air was one of the four elements from which the whole of creation was composed. Aristotle placed it between fire and water in his model of the universe, since he maintained it to be both hot and wet; had he ridden a bike in a climate like Britain's, he'd have known he was only half right. What's indisputable, however, is that for cyclists, the wind is a fundamental part of life: not Shakespeare's 'incorporeal air', but a substantial entity with weight, texture, energy, motion and moods all of its own.

As cyclists, we enjoy a special, complex relationship with the wind. Like sailors and pilots, with whom we have more in common than might be supposed, we are intimately affected by its power, direction and caprices. It's a relationship that, as so often in cycling, has an objective basis in physics, and an entirely subjective one rooted in our experience at any given moment. Put simply, we all love a tailwind, while a headwind poses very particular challenges.

THE INVISIBLE HILL

It is self-evidently more difficult to ride against the wind than to have it at your back: not for nothing, the headwind has been known to generations of cyclists as 'the invisible hill'. And the faster you go, the harder it gets, because, as cyclists, we're subject to one of nature's more inequitable laws, which states that every time your speed doubles, air resistance increases fourfold.

Unkinder still, a pitiless concatenation also means that to go twice as fast means your legs have to produce eight times as much power. If your sole focus is on reaching a destination, or crossing a finishing line, it's easy to regard the wind as an enemy to be beaten – or at least cheated.

But when we ride mindfully, wholly immersed in the journey itself, it's no longer a competition. Indeed, we might usefully see the physical tolls racers pay as the universe telling us it's OK to take things easy.

Because the wind is not an opponent, or some malevolent force out to spoil our fun. It is simply the movement of air between areas of higher and lower pressure. It has no agenda or intent, bears us no ill will. It merely obeys the higher laws of energy and motion: we cannot control it or (whatever the marketing people might tell us) conquer it through clever kit or clothing. What we can do instead is feel it, embrace it and learn from it, as a natural, ever-present part of the ride. In *The Man Who Loved Bicycles*, Daniel Behrman writes: 'You never have the wind with you: either it is against you or you're having a good day.'

MINDFUL OF THE WIND

The mindful cyclist is, nonetheless, a careful student of the wind. Flagpoles, church weathervanes, banks of cloud, the flight of birds and smoke from bonfire and chimney all have much to tell us about its strength and bearing. Routes may be planned so that you ride out into it, when the legs are fresh and the spirit bold, and home with it behind you, to reward and flatter weary limbs with speed conjured literally out of the air. On blustery days, I avoid the main roads with their dangerously unpredictable crosswinds, and explore narrow, sunken lanes, whose high, tree-topped banks provide welcome shelter, just as they did for drovers and other travellers down the centuries. Even the humble hedgerow becomes a battlement to hide behind and gain respite from the onslaught, but mindfulness also means being ready for the sneaky broadside as you pass a drive or gateway.

For now, perhaps, the wind is in your face. It makes you feel as though you're towing a sack of wet sand behind the bike, or a giant is stiff-arming you with his hand against your forehead. Flat roads become hills, hills become mountains, mountains become walls.

All you can do is keep going. You cannot outrun it, reason with it, or make it stop blowing. It knows its own strength, and never grows tired.

Be patient. Turn a corner, and it will swing behind you. In that moment, the whole world is altered. All that thick, treacly air and the elemental forces you've been fighting with now become your allies and friends. You are like a kite cut loose from its string, free to fly, all effort and struggle forgotten, able to savour and revel in your own, miraculous speed.

The Rain it
Raineth

The redoubtable Alfred Wainwright opened the eyes of millions of people – including me – to the glories of England's Lake District through his exquisitely illustrated, handwritten guidebooks. That this beautiful part of the country experiences rain on around 200 days a year was not, in his view, an obstacle to enjoying his beloved hills and footpaths. 'There is no such thing as bad weather,' he famously declared, 'only unsuitable clothing.'

Given the astonishing plethora of waterproof, windproof and thermal kit available now, one might think having 'unsuitable clothing' would no longer be an issue, if not actually impossible, for the cyclist. But like the smiles of Fortune, even today's exotic fibres, fabrics and surface treatments can still flatter to deceive. One soon learns to regard manufacturers' claims for their products with due caution, if not outright scepticism.

In short, no foul-weather gear is without its limitations. For the mindful cyclist, then, this means accepting that part of you (if not most of you) is going to get wet, cold, and probably both, at some stage. Coming to terms with this truth can transform the way you think about the rain. It is no longer something to be avoided or bemoaned, but part of the natural order – and perhaps, in time, something to be actively embraced, even enjoyed.

CAUGHT IN THE RAIN

There are basically two types of wet ride. The first is when we get caught in the rain part way through, having set out in the dry. This is a misfortune that can befall most of us living in temperate climates on almost any day of the year. But it need not be a problem. If we are fully present in the moment, tuned in to the wind, the temperature, the movements of the clouds, smoke from chimneys and the telltale ripples on roadside puddles, we should see it coming. Such observations and awareness connect us once again with the world. They also help us decide what to do next.

The instinctive response, inculcated from childhood, is to get under cover, or put on a coat. It's almost as though we fear getting wet, in case we – what? Rust? Dissolve? Soak up the water like sponges? There is the issue of becoming cold, of course, but on the bike, you can generate your own heat. What we are really grappling with here is not the weather but our own desire – our not-unnatural wish to be dry, warm and, above all, comfortable.

Paradoxically, our attempts to satisfy this desire can have the opposite effect. Trying to avoid or outrun the weather – or simply to get closer to home before it strikes – can involve long detours and/or some hard riding. Put on a jacket too soon, and you can end up wetter from exertion than you would have been from the rain.

Constantly stopping to put on and take off waterproofs adds further time, effort and frustration to the equation. And since getting wet is probably inevitable anyway, it is often better simply to keep going and endure.

CHOOSING THE RAIN

The second, more glorious, kind of wet ride is the one we deliberately set out to do when it's bucketing down already. This, in my view, is to be truly mindful: dressing up and getting on your bike, fully aware of what you're doing and what awaits you, and accepting whatever happens next for itself.

For there is something magnificent, uplifting and empowering about being out in weather that we could easily have chosen to observe from indoors. Riding in a biblical downpour is not especially pleasant, or pleasurable. Neither is it fun in any conventional sense. But it is deeply, viscerally *real*.

On the bike, you're completely encompassed – from above by the rain falling on you, from below by the spray fountaining up from the wheels, and from all sides by the slipstream of passing vehicles. There comes a point – usually fairly swiftly, in my experience – where you physically can't get any wetter. To give in to this, to accept it and embrace it, brings its own kind of pleasure: a physical and mental unshackling from deep-seated inhibitions, fears and prejudices. You are truly at one with the weather, fierce and indomitable, a force of nature in your own right. Any lingering feelings of misery or dejection are banished. You are self-sufficient, truly alive and discovering the true, perhaps unexpected, extent of your own physical and mental resilience.

By accepting whatever the elements throw at us, we grow as cyclists, and as people. It also helps us forge a deeper bond with the bicycle – as true partners, not just fair-weather friends.

On Ascending ... and
Descending

Appealing and logical as it might seem, avoiding hills is a bit like going out only on sunny days: there's nothing wrong with it, but it is to miss out on a crucial dimension of cycling, and life. Hills are the crucibles where we're melted down, refined and forged anew. Plus, unless you happen to live somewhere unusually flat, any road you take will tilt you skywards somewhere along the way.

While hilly terrain is obviously more physically demanding than flat roads, it brings its own joys to the ride. There is real pleasure in exertion, in feeling your muscles working, the air racing in and out of your lungs, your heart beating, your blood surging round. And when you reach the top, there is that opportunity for stillness and reflection, to sense your body settling itself down from its highly charged state, and to gain the perspective that comes with a view from a high place.

Mindful climbing is about concentrating wholly on the here and now. In *Zen and the Art of Motorcycle Maintenance*, Robert M. Pirsig suggests that mountains (or hills, for those in less extreme landscapes) 'should be climbed with as little effort as possible and without desire'. We're conditioned to see hills as obstacles, objects of conquest, and to believe that reaching the top (as fast as possible) is all that really matters. Our goal is external, separate, somewhere up ahead in time and space. We are not truly 'here' because all our energy and focus is 'there'. Is there any state less mindful than that? No wonder it's so physically tiring, and mentally draining.

A CLIMBING MEDITATION

Mindfulness requires us to tune in to one thing – usually our breathing. Happily, this is also the key to riding uphill, so every climb can truly become a meditation.

Regulate your breathing and the legs will find their own rhythm. Feel your diaphragm rising and falling, steady and powerful. Try consciously 'inhaling' the road, physically pulling it towards you with each in-breath, then use the out-breath to push yourself forward. Be aware of the wheels rotating: all must be smooth and circular, without edges or angles.

As in yoga, maintaining a steady, focused gaze ahead aids concentration. Fix your eyes on a spot on the road about a bike's-length ahead, and what lies beyond ceases to exist, or matter.

A long, slow climb is also an opportunity to appreciate nature on her own level, and at her own pace. In spring, the steep banks that line many of my local lanes are overflowing with bluebells, stitchwort, celandines, windflowers, cow parsley, jack-by-the-hedge, orchids – a veritable Titania's bower. There are sandstone outcrops, too, craggy as canyons in a Western, roped with the exposed, knotted roots of oak, ash and beech trees, and dotted with rabbit warrens like the portholes in a wooden ship. As Pirsig also points out: 'It's the sides of the mountain that sustain life, not the top.'

And sometimes, the best and most comfortable way to reach the top is simply to take the bike for a walk instead. Even the professionals would agree.

GLORY IN DESCENDING

To every action there is an equal and opposite reaction – what goes up must come down, and there is a special glory in descending. The sheer delight of all that free, effortless speed is matched only by the delicious thrill of being on the edge of control and common sense, which captivated us in childhood and never really leaves us. We may still fall short of flying, but the bike can bring us closer to it than almost anything else.

Yet even in this exquisite state of grace, focus is required – nay, essential. As speed rises, so the margins of error contract. To descend mindfully is to cross the magical threshold from simply riding the road to reading it; not only knowing precisely where you are, but also sensing and predicting what might be coming next. Conscious thought is too slow and laborious. At 25 miles per hour, one second's pondering takes you 40 feet further down the road.

But to ride fast down a smooth, twisting road you know well is a transcendent experience. Slashing through a corner in a seamless, fluid movement is cycling's equivalent of hitting the high note or a hole-in-one. String a series of such corners together, and bike and rider flow down the hill like a raindrop on a windowpane.

To spend time in the hills or mountains is an exquisite mix of effort and exhilaration, steady progress and glorious speed. It is a mirror to the human condition – and the very essence of what it means to ride a bike.

Finding **the Upside**
of Punctures

Few things are more dispiriting for the cyclist than a puncture – especially in the back wheel. A sudden, spongy vagueness in the handling is swiftly followed by the soul-sapping burble of metal rim and flaccid rubber on pavement, which sounds suspiciously like deep, mocking laughter. At best, you're looking at lost time and some strenuous, messy alfresco toil; at worst, a long walk, or the ignominy of having to be rescued.

To observe and accept this turn of events without judgement demands a singular effort of will, the more so if it's raining. (For me, acceptance comes after an involuntary exclamation of shock and disappointment, and a few good, deep breaths.) However, I've slowly learned that a flat can be a kind of meditation, and bring new and positive insights into the cycling life.

For instance, consider how amazingly frequently punctures don't happen. In a typical year, I'll get about three; an average of one every 90 rides or so. I'll take those odds. A few millimetres of rubber stand between the precious, pressurized air that makes cycling possible, and the numberless sharp objects trying to rob us of it. That these often unseen enemies succeed so rarely is almost miraculous – yet we take our tyres' ability to repel them almost entirely for granted.

MEDITATION ON A PUNCTURE

Prevention is, of course, vastly preferable to cure. We must be aware of, then avoid where possible, the flints, thorns, nails, potholes, raised edges, bits of glass and other agents of woe that await us. It's to hear the distant whine and clang of the farmer's rotary flail hedge cutter, and seek another way; to run good tyres, properly inflated, and change them if they're cut, cracked or threadbare. Above all, it's to ride with eyes and ears wide open. And when (not if) the dreaded moment arrives, framing what follows as a meditation can draw at least some of the sting.

Removing a wheel is a chance to reacquaint ourselves with a bike's vital components, which meld simplicity and robustness with intricacy and precision so elegantly that one can almost forgive them their grease and grime. It also reveals otherwise hidden parts of the frame; an ideal moment to inspect for damage or accumulated dirt to address at greater leisure. Plus, we can appreciate anew the wheel itself – in engineering terms, the strongest structure ever invented, able to support more than 100 times its own weight, and resist huge lateral and torsional forces generated in accelerating, braking and turning.

RESTORING SELF-SUFFICIENCY

Perhaps most importantly, dealing with a puncture restores a sense of self-reliance and self-sufficiency we're rapidly losing in today's hi-tech world. Any automotive problem more serious than a flat battery usually means a trip to the local garage: similarly, if something shuts down or goes haywire in your phone, computer or washing-machine, it almost inevitably requires professional intervention.

A puncture is one thing we're still able to fix ourselves, using basic tools and inexpensive parts we can carry with us. Sore thumbs, oil-stains and arriving home a bit later than planned are a small price to pay for the warm sense of self-sufficiency that comes from getting yourself and your faithful companion back on the road. From disaster, triumph; from defeat, victory; from despair, hope and faith renewed.

THE KINDNESS OF STRANGERS

But not all of us have the tools, strength, aptitude or inclination to be our own mechanic. I dread flats on my vintage bike, since removing a wheel means entirely disconnecting, then reconnecting, the brakes (the hub gear too, if it's the rear) and requires three separate spanners in three different sizes. And most long-haul cyclists (myself included) can ruefully recall the day they suffered three punctures, having set off cheerfully thinking two spare inner-tubes would be plenty…

On such occasions, the bicycle prompts us to reach out to family and friends – or to trust in the kindness of strangers. In the time I spent waiting for my father to arrive with car and bike rack after a recent puncture on my vintage machine (thanks, Dad), two riders pulled over and offered their help. Any cyclist worthy of the name will do the same, even if it's just to hold your bike, pass you things and provide moral support while you put in the hard graft. Even in the cauldron of professional racing, riders will wait and allow a rival to rejoin the fray after a crash, flat or mechanical incident. As cyclists, we are all part of a family of millions – and are also keenly aware that the situation may be reversed one day.

Punctures are an inevitable, if unwelcome, part of cycling. But regarded mindfully, they are opportunities for learning and growth, keeping us – literally – grounded, and in touch with the realities of cycling life.

The Weight
of the World

Archimedes claimed that given a lever long enough and a fulcrum on which to place it, he would move the world. What a shame he was born a couple of millennia too soon to ride a bike. Because with our simple machine (of which I think he would most wholeheartedly approve), we cyclists boldly engage with the most powerful, fundamental forces on Earth.

Every bike ride, taken mindfully, is a direct, hands-on physics lesson. Had I understood this when I was younger, I might have stuck with the subject. Now, in adulthood, the abstract concepts and tangled formulae I tried (and largely failed) to grasp in those far-off dusty classrooms have become very real indeed. The bicycle, which provides such a feeling of freedom, is subject to laws so ironclad and immutable they govern every moving object there is, and has ever been. Behind its art and poetry lies the rigid legislation of classical mechanics, codified by Sir Isaac Newton, and under whose stern jurisdiction we still labour.

LAWS OF PHYSICS

Take inertia, for instance. From the Latin *iners*, meaning idle or sluggish, it's the resistance of a physical object to any change in its state of motion. It is inertia you must first overcome to set your stationary bicycle moving, by applying a force to it: the heavier the bike and rider, the harder it is to get going.

And we all know, instinctively and unconsciously, what gravity is. As long as dropped objects fall unerringly to the floor, and we don't find ourselves floating off into the blue, we don't afford it a moment's thought. Get on a bike, however, and we are suddenly only too aware of gravity's absolute hold over us. On the flat, it's relatively benign, and goes pretty much unnoticed. But when the road tilts, it drops the whole weight of the world into your back pocket.

The same goes for air resistance, or aerodynamic drag. Most of the time, it doesn't affect us because we're either moving too slowly (as pedestrians) or letting machinery deal with it (as drivers or passengers). Again, the bike reveals just how wide of the mark Shakespeare was when he gave us the phrase 'thin air'.

Trundling along at 10 miles an hour, the effect of air resistance on your forward progress is almost imperceptible, since it's equal to other forces such as friction between your tyres and the road. But once you reach 20 miles an hour and above, overcoming air resistance will account for between 70 and 90 per cent of your effort. What's more, the faster you go, the more reluctant it is to let you through.

In fact, there's barely a line in Newton's canon that doesn't apply to bike and rider. It may not feel like it, but you're not losing energy as you go along: you're converting it from one form into another, neither creating nor destroying it. To the action of pedalling uphill there's the equal and opposite reaction of gravity trying to drag you back down again. And as you work, you produce heat. To arrive home dripping with sweat and legs like jelly is merely a mark of fealty to the laws of thermodynamics. And thanks to Sir Isaac, the traffic isn't all one way: he also grants us the effortless speed of a long plunge downhill, and the glorious relief of turning a corner and finding the wind's behind us at last. Physics giveth, as well as taketh away.

CONNECT WITH THE FORCES

But while we are inevitably, inextricably tied to these great laws, the bicycle ensures we aren't wholly enslaved by them. Though we may never escape them, we may find freedom within them.

Ernest Hemingway, who knew a thing or two about titanic struggles, wrote: 'It is by riding a bicycle that you learn the contours of a country best, since you have to sweat up the hills and coast down them.' Ride a road you habitually drive, and you'll find it's nowhere near as flat as you thought. With our cars, aircraft and other vehicles, we've become disconnected from the forces that govern our world. The bicycle reminds us of their presence, and gives us a deeper sense of our place in the universe, in terms of our insignificance, and our oneness with everything around us. And to challenge the physical laws is to gain a new perspective on the human powers and constructs that often weigh on us so heavily.

Feel the weight of the world as you turn it beneath your wheels. It will bring new appreciation for forces we learned about in school and have taken for granted (assuming we've thought about them) ever since. And for this moment at least, everything else will seem easy.

Cleaning
the Bike

When it comes to my car, I faithfully attend to the basic, common-sense, safety-critical stuff: regular servicing, maintaining correct tyre pressures and fluid levels, replacing worn wiper blades, that kind of thing. Cosmetically, though, good enough is good enough.

The same applies to my bikes. They're not pristine: they are, after all, high-mileage machines that work outside in all weathers. They are not ornaments, or precious works of art meant only to be looked at. A bike without a mark on it hasn't seen much of the world, and to my mind, a bicycle that isn't ridden is as melancholy as an unread book, or a Stradivarius kept locked up in a bank vault.

But while I don't – and, realistically, can't – keep them in showroom condition, I get distracted and jumpy if they're really filthy. This is partly because I can see a direct connection between cleanliness and safety when it comes to the bike, whose brakes, transmission and major bearings are all exposed to the elements. Plus, I know of no component manufacturer that deliberately designs its products to squeak, grate, grind or crunch.

THE HORSE THAT NEEDS NO HAY

It's also partly due to principles I learned in my teenage years, when I was fortunate enough to ride horses as well as bikes. Among the many rules drummed into me by a succession of formidable instructors was that you owed it to your horse to be properly turned out. It was, I was sternly informed, a serious faux pas to turn up to ride with muddy boots, or leave the yard with bits of straw from the stable still stuck in your horse's tail. Such oversights, though seemingly trivial, were deemed to show a lack of care and respect for your equine partner, and hinted darkly at a deeper negligence. Today, I feel the same lurking shame about a grimy chain or greasy thumbprint.

In similar vein, I was also taught that after a ride, you always take care of your horse first, then yourself; never mind that it's dark, freezing cold, pouring with rain, and the last thing you ate was a slice of toast 15 hours ago. So thoroughly inculcated was this honourable and selfless ideal that I still apply it to my bikes today. Before going indoors, I'll give the whole thing a quick wipe down and re-lube, even when my shoes are full of water and my fingers have gone numb. And if this throwback to my equestrian past appears fanciful, it's worth noting that early marketing campaigns in rural France promoted the bicycle as 'the horse that needs no hay'.

LITTLE AND OFTEN

Everyone has their own idea of what constitutes an acceptable state of cleanliness. Cosmetic considerations aside, cleaning the bike affords a valuable opportunity to check for damage and wear and tear. It needn't be a full-scale, take-everything-apart clean, either. A frayed cable, cut or threadbare tyres, a loose spoke, brake pads worn to wafers, a stretched chain, play in the hubs or headset – all can be revealed in the course of a quick once-over. Five minutes with a rag and a can of water-displacing spray at the end of the ride today could save a long walk home tomorrow.

Cleaning a bike is a bit like cleaning a bathroom. Do it every day, and it's a quick, simple, painless job: do it every couple of months and it's a whole different prospect. I have to confess I don't enjoy cleaning bikes enough to want to spend hours on it, so the little-and-often approach works for me. That said, I find there's something truly meditative in doing a thorough, deep clean now and again. Getting into all the bike's myriad nooks and crannies requires dexterity and patience. It also fosters a deeper understanding of how the machine is put together, and the interplay of its parts and systems – an intimacy that deepens and enriches the relationship. It is the path to 'a' bike becoming 'your' bike.

For me, though, the clincher is that a bike that's clean and running quietly just feels smoother, more 'together' somehow. The effect is purely psychological, of course, but no less real and potent for that. In fact, so much of cycling is in the mind that we should never underestimate the power of these little illusions. Wheeling out a shiny bicycle is like putting on a crisp new shirt, or stepping out of the front door on a sharp spring morning. Everything is bright. Anything is possible.

Adventures
by Night

Not everyone has a choice about riding in the dark. For regular commuters in higher latitudes, it's a fact of life for large portions of the year; for those of us with day jobs, going out at night is the only way to get a ride in during the working week in winter.

I put in many a moonlit mile when my daughter was small. By the time I'd finished work, bathed her and read innumerable bedtime stories, the day was long over, and I had no option but to take to the lanes tooled up with halogen lights and high-vis clothing. My brother-in-law, 10 years or so behind me, is now doing the same, heading out into the woods on his mountain bike when my nephews and niece are (finally) tucked up in bed.

To ride at night without these imperatives, however, seems contrary. Even in broad daylight, as cyclists we often seem to be invisible to drivers – and potholes, thorns and other puncture hazards aren't always easy to avoid, even when you can see them coming. So the jeopardy is vastly multiplied in darkness, especially on unfamiliar roads. I once rode a 400 kilometre event that involved riding through the night in territory I'd never previously visited. The experience of plunging down a steep, winding lane by the fitful light of a single 150-candlepower bulb still haunts me years later.

THE HOURS OF DARKNESS

As any Victorian novel or TV costume drama attests, our ancestors lived in a much darker world than we do. We're permanently bathed in our streetlights, car headlamps and omnipresent glowing screens, so much so that those of us who live in towns suffer from light pollution, and have almost forgotten what the night sky really looks like. We may have shaken off our irrational fears of ghosts and other things that go bump in the night, but we are also less attuned to and comfortable with the darkness than we once were.

As a result, we still place a block between ourselves and a large part of our world, and our lives. We see the hours of darkness as limiting, restrictive – even useless. In so doing, we voluntarily reduce both our cycling time, and our connection with a side of the human experience that has shaped us and our thinking since the beginning of time.

CAUGHT BETWEEN WORLDS

To ride in the dark is to find ourselves between worlds, crossing a strange hinterland that's neither entirely part of today, nor wholly belonging to tomorrow. The day is done, darkness is telling us to stop, rest and sleep – yet here we are, fully awake and alert as owls in a demi-monde full of excitement, intrigue and possibility. We can rediscover the sense of excitement and freedom we had as children when we took to the streets after dark to go trick-or-treating or carol-singing. And in its very irrationality and contrariness, there is also a sense of rebellion and empowerment, of reclaiming something we've learned (or been told) is no longer ours.

In this space, out of time and mind, the imagination can go to work. Riding through a tunnel of trees on a windy night under a full moon, I feel like the highwayman Dick Turpin on his epic flight to York, a messenger rushing urgent dispatches to a fretful HQ, or the Scarlet Pimpernel galloping out of revolutionary Paris, leaving his baffled, frustrated pursuers cursing far behind. Others have described it as like being in an incredibly immersive video game. To each their own.

A MINDFUL ESCAPADE
But to balance these fantastical allusions, night-riding also calls for awareness of an especially high order. The first focus must be on preparations: high-visibility clothing, the bike lit up like a pinball machine, and brakes, tyres and everything else in good working order.

Once under way, let your attention be on the road surface itself. Good lights, and sticking to roads you know well, are the best guarantees of avoiding sharps and potholes.

With our vision reduced, our other senses become keener at night. We tune in to the texture of the air, more like a clear, refreshing fluid than the day's mere assembly of vapours – colder, denser and filled with scents: damp grass, wood smoke, approaching rain. The sound of the wind is magnified, roaring in the trees like a big surf: when it drops, you can catch distant church bells and passing trains, the hoot of an owl, the vixen's shriek.

A mindful escapade by night has a power and magic all of its own. It is a meditative state, in which the world shrinks down to the cone of light in front of you: peripheral sights and distractions are almost entirely eliminated. The sensation of speed is also magnified enormously. It's as though gravity has been turned down a notch; everything, including the mind, feels lighter, freer, more fluid. It is a ticket to another world.

So, what are you doing tonight?

Birds and Beasts

I love cycling above almost everything else. Nothing, save sheet ice, serious illness or an immovable deadline, will keep me from it. Yet I will stop mid-ride to watch a bird or animal that catches my eye. In that moment, cycling comes second.

Although I'm not a naturalist, to encounter 'the wild' unlooked-for in the course of its normal daily round is precious to me, and the perfect mindful state. The world stops. Time ceases to have any measure or meaning. I can truly forget where, and even

who, I am. All other thought and sensory awareness is suspended. And when the event is over, I have a very real sense of coming back from somewhere distant, beautiful – and, I think, better.

TRULY IN NATURE

The bike connects us to the natural world almost as intimately as walking – with the added bonus that it enables us to see more of it in a given time. On the bike, we're part of the landscape, not merely passing through it; we have full use of senses we're deprived of in the car. We are truly in nature, not insulated from it. It's almost as though animals and birds understand that we pose no threat to them, and therefore accept us into their world. And since our approach is silent, we can get much closer to them before they realize we're there.

I've had some magical animal encounters where we've simply sat (or stood) and considered one another, without fear or prejudice, across the chasm between our species and universes. Riding between high banks, I've glanced up and looked a stoat or snake straight in the eye; on quiet lanes, I've stopped to hold lengthy, wordless conferences with foxes. Reynard's reputation is for cunning, but I admire him for his insouciance and boldness: a brazen, careless fellow in his rich red coat.

HARMONY WITH BIRDS OF PREY

Of all the wild creatures I encounter on the road, the birds of prey are my favourites. I see buzzards regularly when I'm cycling; it thrills me to have these large, yellow-eyed, razor-taloned raptors with their five-foot wingspan, living so close to me. The kestrel is another familiar sight, hovering over the fields, while glimpses of his reclusive brother, the sparrowhawk, and their transient, mysterious cousins, the merlin and hobby, are rare, exquisite treats. I find their economy, focus and purity of purpose truly exhilarating. I love their swiftness and efficiency, the way they slice soundlessly and almost invisibly through the countryside – much as we cyclists do.

My ultimate prize, however, is the barn owl. The sight of this pale ghost patrolling the meadows at dusk will, quite literally, stop me in my tracks. On a couple of privileged occasions, I've even found myself riding along with this silent, spectral predator cruising just above and ahead of me, holding formation for a hundred yards or more. Such moments are uplifting and humbling, impossible to arrange and never to be forgotten.

NATURE'S REWARDS

It is uncanny how often nature rewards me for taking a longer, harder route, going out at an odd time, or braving poor weather, with a sight I would not otherwise have seen. On consecutive days, spontaneous detours recently presented me with a big brown hare running across a field of young wheat, and the first pair of red kites I've ever seen in this part of the world. Such meetings justify the extra time and effort a hundredfold.

For the mindful cyclist, being aware of wildlife is part of creating and maintaining a connection with the world and the seasons. Migrant birds tell me more surely than any calendar that the seasons are shifting: some arrive as harbingers of winter, while others bring summer with them from distant lands, and take it away again when they depart.

We are privileged to share their space and freedom, breathe their air, feel their sun and rain, and savour stolen glimpses of their hidden lives. They remind us that we are all part of the same living world, and finding our own way through it.

Riding in
Traffic

Paying attention is one of the underlying themes of mindfulness; focusing on the present moment – the here and now – is the hook on which the practice ultimately hangs. And it is never more critical than when you're riding in traffic.

Any time that cars and bicycles meet, absolutely the last thing you need is your mind wandering. Cycling mindfully in traffic is precisely the opposite of detaching from the world. It's about engaging eyes, ears and instincts – the conscious part of your brain can deal with the inflow of sensory information, but it is your unconscious that will get you through a gap that, if you stopped to think about it, would literally not be there.

And what about those inevitable occasions where a driver doesn't give you enough room? When they pass you six inches from your elbow, into the path of an oncoming bus, halfway round a blind corner, or on a narrow country road? This is when your state of mindfulness can, quite literally, save your life.

ACCEPTING THE MOMENT

In these moments (and I've had many of them), I feel the universe, and life itself, shrink down. Everything I am, know and feel is compressed into a space just a few inches wide and a million miles long, outside which nothing else exists. It is a fragment of time in which everything can change, or nothing. The margins are so small it's impossible to think about them: in the time it took to frame them, it might already be too late. All I can do is focus my attention on where I am and what I'm doing. In this minutely focused state, the brain shifts into warp drive, analysing data, running through scenarios, formulating and discarding options at fantastic speed. I've sometimes returned to the scene of a terrifying near-death experience, which seemed at the time to extend over leagues and aeons, and almost missed it because I blinked.

Mindfulness is about accepting the moment without prejudice: what is, is, and nothing more. Riding in traffic requires an acceptance, however hard it seems, that even if we do everything right, every time, one day that might not be enough. It is, perhaps, the hardest lesson the bike has to teach us.

But acceptance is not the same as fatalism, and awareness need not become paranoia. They give us a framework in which to operate, and freedom to choose how we respond. If you believe in divine protection, you may wish to invoke it. Most deities, however, would also point out that they have granted us enough intelligence to take steps to protect ourselves. I venture no opinion on the wearing of helmets, but I strongly advocate wearing bright colours in all conditions, and being lit up like a Christmas tree when venturing out after dark.

SIXTH SENSE

I apologize if this seems a very technical, functional kind of mindfulness. It's urgent, steely, imperative, rather than relaxing or meditative.

But it is mindfulness nonetheless. It's about paying attention to your position on the road, for example. The mindful cyclist does not hug the gutter, and knows – indeed, expects – that the door of the next parked car could open right in front of them. Remaining non-judgemental after being forced into the kerb by an eighteen-wheeler or carved up by a speeding SUV is extraordinarily hard, yet it is just a moment. A horrible one, to be sure, but that's all it is. (Unless there is real malice, in which case get their number.) The impulse to yell and scream and want to hit back is perfectly natural: adrenaline and cortisol are only obeying orders. This, too, will – and must – pass.

Over time, this awareness can develop into a kind of sixth sense. After more than 20 years on the road, I can generally tell not only what kind of vehicle is approaching me from behind but also whether it will give me ample, enough, too little or no room as it passes, just by its sound. Intuition and experience are good friends to have along for the ride.

For most of us, dealing with traffic and all its many challenges forms an inevitable part of the cycling life. As cyclists, we are part of the solution, but we still have a long way to go. For now, we must be constantly aware, embrace the realities of the roads as a shared space – and be the change we wish to see in the world.

The Road Goes Ever
On and On

The number 100 has a strange fascination about it – a certain 'rightness' or completeness. To reach 100 years of age, for example, is a universal landmark, whether for an individual or an organization. And for cyclists, there is a powerful mystique about the ride of 100 miles or kilometres, known as the 'century'.

To complete that first century is a rite of passage: the moment when one crosses an invisible threshold and becomes a cyclist, rather than someone who merely rides a bike. It's a qualification that can never be taken away – in the same way that a rider who finishes the Tour de France, even if he's flat dead last, can forever call himself 'a Giant of the Road'.

The century is a talisman because it's a simple, identifiable and unarguable measure, even to non-cyclists. What constitutes a 'long ride' is far more subjective. Fifty miles sounds reasonably daunting, yet as countless charity events prove, it's well within most people's compass, even if the bike remains untouched the other 364 days a year. By the same token, most of us would balk at riding 190 miles in one day, yet that's exactly what the pros do in the classic race from Milan to San Remo – and in seven hours or less.

QUALITY, NOT QUANTITY

Distance rarely tells the whole story of a ride. The ascent of Alpe d'Huez, in France, is less than nine miles long; Mont Ventoux is just over 13. The Arenberg Forest sector of Paris–Roubaix is a trifling mile-and-a-half. All routinely leave hardened pros openly shattered in body and mind.

Hence racers always measure their rides in duration (usually hours), not distance. They'll also confirm that

the toughest challenge in cycling – if not all of sport –
is the Hour Record. Uniquely, it's not about who
can cover a set distance the fastest, but who can ride
furthest in a fixed time. The Belgian racer Eddy Merckx,
who broke the record in 1972, swore it was the hardest
thing he ever did on a bike, and reckoned it took four
years off his life expectancy.

What we're really talking about is relativity. Einstein
famously summed it up thus: 'Put your hand on a hot
stove for a minute, and it seems like an hour. Sit with
a pretty girl for an hour, and it seems like a minute.'
Or: ride a century with your best friend on a summer's
day and it feels like a spin round the block. Ride round
the block alone in a hailstorm and get three punctures,
and it feels like 100 miles.

So we should seek always to define our rides in
terms of quality, not quantity. To focus on distance is
to project ourselves to some unseen point down the
road, rather than being fully aware of the road we're
travelling right now. Fixating on the fact that you still

have however-many miles to go won't help you get up this hill, round that tricky corner. The other danger is that if you set out to cover a certain mileage and don't manage it, you perceive the ride (and possibly yourself, too) as a failure.

EVER MINDFUL

To remain mindful on a long trip, especially alone, can be desperately hard. A niggling noise or slight discomfort can become all-consuming. It is made much easier by ensuring the bike is in good order, and that both it and you are properly equipped. Fifty miles in the rain is hard enough without leaving your waterproofs or pump at home.

The mindful cyclist is also keenly aware of what the body is telling him or her, and refuels regularly. A long ride burns up the body's glycogen stores, which provide energy to the muscles. Once these reserves are gone, they're running on empty. The result is a sudden, spectacular implosion known rather quaintly to

Anglophone cyclists as the 'hunger knock' or the 'bonk', and to our French colleagues as, somewhat fancifully, 'the witch with green teeth' or, rather more graphically, 'meeting the man with the hammer'. Not an acquaintance you want to make, believe me.

To have nothing to do but ride the bike, and all day to do it, is a pleasure to be savoured. If that's your happy lot today, take the sounds, sights, smells and sensations and store them up like bright golden pennies against shorter, duller days to come. Set yourself no targets for speed or distance. It is quality, not quantity, that counts.

Riding Together...
and Alone

Cycling is one of those rare sports for which you don't
need teammates, a partner or an opponent. The basic
activity and equipment are the same whether you're
taking to the road solo, or with thousands of others
on a charity ride. The choice to go alone or in
company is thus entirely yours to make,
according to your mood and ambitions.
But from a mindfulness perspective,
there are some important
differences.

At any given point
in my cycling career,
I've always been lucky

enough to have one good riding partner. And there's a lot to be said for finding someone compatible with whom to share experiences, knowledge, new roads and good times.

When you're both strong, you can push each other to go further and faster than you would alone. You take turns riding at the front in the wind, and fixing a flat or mechanical problem becomes a shared endeavour. Etiquette and common sense require you to go at the pace of the slowest, so you must be aware of your partner's state of mind and being, as well as your own. You tune in to each other's strengths and weaknesses, matching your efforts to mutual benefit. It encourages a kind of collective, corporate mindfulness: a wider, more encompassing awareness, not focusing solely on oneself.

POWER IN NUMBERS

This becomes even more crucial when riding in a group. You must be constantly, acutely aware of your position relative to your companions: a touch of wheels, elbows or handlebars can bring everyone down in a whirling tangle of bodies, limbs and unyielding hardware. You must also judge the pace correctly, neither slowing the group down nor shelling people off the back – and, of course, take your turns in the wind. It's tight, concentrated, fast and fluid, and takes time and nerve to perfect.

The rewards can be stunning. Riding in someone's slipstream, known as drafting, reduces your required effort by around a quarter, allowing groups to sustain much higher speeds over much longer distances than soloists. For a while, I rode with an informal team, and experienced the amazing potential of aggregated effort. On one memorable day, with a tailwind and everyone working seamlessly together, I looked down at my bike computer and saw we were flying along at almost 40 miles per hour. All you could hear was the low, hollow roar of hard racing tyres on tarmac, the whirr of chains and the hiss of stiff aluminium rims through the air. A magical, inspirational sound: the music of motion and human power.

ALONE, BUT NOT LONELY

Riding solo, by contrast, we can set our own pace, find our own rhythm. There's no slowing or waiting, no trying to keep up, no comments or conversation to divert and distract the attention. We can concentrate fully on what we're doing, and the moment as we perceive it. This, to me, is liberty in its purest and sweetest form.

I remember vividly the day when, aged about eight, I was permitted to ride round the block on my own for the first time. It was a heady cocktail of excitement, anticipation, nervousness and resolve. I was completely alone – yet I wasn't lonely; instead, I positively revelled in my new-found solitude and freedom. For me, that was a moment of liberation and infinite possibility, when I suddenly became aware that once you were on the road, you could keep going more or less forever. Forty years later, I still get the same feeling every time I go out.

The bike is one of the few places where, if we wish, we can be left alone. Even at home, the phone rings, people come to the door, and partners, children and pets demand our attention, while unpaid bills and undone chores eye us accusingly. When we ride, these things can come with us only if we invite them.

On the road alone, we are our sole source of motivation and inspiration. There's no one to encourage us as we toil up that hill, cheer us as we speed down the other side, or pat us on the back when we return. We have complete control over our own destiny, but to exercise it, we must be constantly aware of ourselves. Riding mindfully means sensing when it's time to head home, then doing so – or that you've still got gas in the tank, and the will to burn it. And whoever you ride with, the bike is always there, as an enabler, partner and extension of yourself. Which means you'll never be left to fend entirely for yourself.

Mental Strength
and Physical Power

Cycling is hard work – at least, if you plan to go any distance, at any speed, in any terrain that isn't as flat as a table. So physical strength and fitness are obviously important. They're also among the main reasons many of us start, and stick with, cycling in the first place.

Very often, cycling is reduced to a knock-down, drag-out contest between ourselves and the forces of nature – gravity, inertia, friction, air resistance and rolling resistance. To an extent, this is true. The basic technique is simple, and the laws of physics mean the more power you can produce, the faster you can go. But the beauty of cycling is that it's not solely dependent on brute strength. It's also a mind game.

PLAY THE LONG GAME

Getting fitter and stronger is, in itself, a good thing. Apart from the health benefits, it broadens our range and expands our horizons. For me, it's about being confident I can tackle any terrain I might encounter, and not having to avoid a given route because of a particular hill. And if, perchance, I wake up with a fancy to put in 50 hard miles today, I know it's within my compass.

But riding well, and ensuring you're still doing so years from now, is less about the raw power you can expend and more about how efficiently you can use it. As cyclists, we must play the long game. That means being attuned to how much effort we're putting in. In search of a 'good workout', many of us end up riding a bit too hard, most of the time (guilty as charged). Ironically, this can leave us stuck on a plateau, never getting any stronger or faster. We become like an elastic band kept permanently at full stretch: when we need to extend ourselves just a little further – to make it over a particularly steep climb, or put in an extra-long day – there's nothing left.

TUNE IN TO YOUR LEGS

We need to let go of the 'no pain, no gain' mantra that pervades life, not just sport – the deathly notion that, somehow, if it doesn't hurt, you're not trying hard enough, and won't see the best results. As long as you can get up that hill somehow – even if it means walking part of the way – that's all that counts. How fast you do it is utterly unimportant (unless you're racing, of course).

Yet we must also be aware that *some* effort is required. Our muscles enlarge and strengthen only when we ask them to do more than they're currently capable of. Not Nietzsche's 'that which does not kill us makes us stronger', exactly, but we must break them down (carefully) in order to build them up. So tune in to your legs as you ride. Focus on your perceived effort – how hard you feel you're working. Could you sustain this effort all day? Recognize when you're asking your body for extra power – on a hill, for example – and how easily it can provide it (or not).

The great Italian *campione* of the 1960s and '70s, Felice Gimondi, said: 'Basic physical strength is necessary. But you need to have a little imagination, to be intelligent and calm. You need mental control. It is self-control.' And, he might have added, you need to be fully in the moment, not worrying about what could happen, or might lie ahead.

OBSERVE AND ACCEPT

One of cycling's most oft-quoted truisms is that whether you think you can, or you think you can't, you'll be right. In other words, the moment the head starts questioning whether you can get up this hill/maintain this pace/ manage another five miles against this headwind, the legs lose all their impetus, and you're suddenly struggling.

This is emphatically not a manifesto for positive thinking. As anyone who's ever tried to quit smoking, lose weight or do anything else requiring self-inflicted physical deprivation will testify, willpower is unreliable and overrated. The challenge is to not think about whether we can or can't, and merely observe and accept the moment as and for what it is.

On the bike, our psychological strength is constantly assayed and refined. A long, steep climb (or even a short, steep one), a relentless headwind, the cold, the heat, the rain: all can be as mentally demoralizing as they are physically exhausting. In fact, it's often the will that gives up first.

But cycling trains the mind, as well as the body, making it stronger and more resilient. Overcoming hills, bad weather, mechanical problems, close encounters with cars – all require us to draw on our reserves of fortitude, patience, hardiness and courage. Just as exceeding our muscles' capacity makes them stronger, so stretching our mental resources helps them grow in size and power – a training that equips us for life itself.

Riding
Off-road

These days, it's easy to forget that at one time, *all* cyclists were off-roaders, since there were no roads to be on. (It's another overlooked fact that in both Britain and America, it was cyclists, not motorists, who first lobbied their governments to make improving the highways a national priority.) But with traffic volumes ever increasing, the appeal of leaving the tarmac behind is obvious, and technology now allows mountain bikes and their intrepid riders to reach places even goats would think twice about.

Riding on the road generally requires us to be entirely immersed in what the traffic is doing: it's difficult, and hazardous, to give our attention to much else. Heading off-road allows us to refocus completely. With no cars to consider, we can be fully attuned to ourselves, our surroundings, the sounds and textures of the trail, birdsong, sunshine, the scent and quality of the air. We're also free to revel in the workings of our limbs, lungs and heart – and if it's wet, indulge in the childhood pleasure of playing in the mud and getting filthy under the sensible, grown-up guise of sport and exercise. As the English Romantic poet William Blake puts it: 'Great things are done when men and mountains meet.'

And Blake's use of the verb 'meet' is pivotal here. We apply it in the context of friends, colleagues and minds – and also of targets, objectives and opponents. So it's important that we approach the mountain (or hill, or forest, or anywhere else) in the appropriate state of mind.

GUESTS OF NATURE

At a dedicated trail centre, with its purpose-built, graded runs, to view our meeting as a squaring-up, staring-down kind of encounter is OK. The challenges

we face here – jumps, berms, boardwalks, drop-offs
– are the products of human imagination: artifice built
on natural foundations with the deliberate intent of
testing our skills and nerve. Nature is generous, and
will join us in our games with grace and good humour,
allowing herself to be wrestled and overthrown like a
large, affectionate dog romping with a boisterous child.

But in the mountains, hills, forests and byways, we
are her guests. Though we are vastly less intrusive than
anything with an engine, we still bring alien wheels,
metals and mechanisms into her domain. We should
approach this meeting, then, with a degree of reverence
and humility. If we hammer through the country without
seeing, hearing, thinking or feeling, we are not visitors
but intruders, and risk missing – or even destroying –
the very things we came out here to find.

We are also unlikely to be the only people nature is
entertaining today. Although the road is nominally a
shared space where everyone has equal status, it certainly
doesn't feel that way to most cyclists. The outdoors,

though, emphatically is. In my part of the world, we coexist with walkers of the serious-long-distance, Sunday-afternoon and dog-accompanying variety, picnickers, families, birdwatchers, hang gliders, kite-fliers, runners and horse riders – to say nothing of the resident livestock and wildlife. They must be part of our awareness and acceptance too – just as we would wish to be part of theirs.

BE IN AND WITH NATURE

With their sophisticated suspension, braking and transmission systems, mountain bikes allow us to tackle almost any terrain. They enable us to go further, faster, and to more extreme locations. But they also, to some degree, insulate us from the rough surfaces, steep gradients and natural hazards that make off-road riding what it is. Too much technology can make us little more than operators, while creating a sense of invincibility and entitlement that detaches us from the moment. If we are too focused on doing our own 'great things', we are not in and with nature; we're seeking to control and co-opt her for our own ends. The desire to explore new territory is a primal human urge that riding off-road allows us to satisfy in ourselves. But we must also be alive to our equally hardwired instincts to possess, exploit and conquer what we find.

Going off-road provides a sanctuary from the frenetic pace of life, and the crush of traffic. The bike is an enabler, taking us further than our feet alone. It connects us to the earth, air and sky, and can, depending on the surface, literally shake us into a deeper awareness of ourselves. And even if, like me, you live hundreds of miles from the nearest mountain, there are great things to be done when we meet nature, whatever form she takes, on the right terms, and with due respect.

Shift in Focus

When we were kids, how many gears your bike had was an important bragging right. More was obviously better – a notion that tends to stay with us, and in more aspects of life than just cycling. As adults, many of us are inclined to make gears something of a fetish. Today, you can buy a bike with anything up to 33 gears (3 chain-rings up front, 11 sprockets behind): if you have the means, you can run pro-grade kit with carbon fibre and titanium parts to save weight, ceramic bearings for smoothness and durability, and electric shifters that operate wirelessly. Even more modest offerings are robust, reliable, easy to adjust and so intuitive a child can master them in five minutes flat.

All of which probably has Henri Desgrange, who in 1903 created the Tour de France to promote his *L'Auto* newspaper, turning in his grave. Irascible and dictatorial, as well as publicity hungry, Desgrange deliberately set out to make his race as inhumanly demanding as possible. To this end, he resolutely forbade the use of derailleurs at the Tour until 1937. 'I still feel that variable gears are only for people over 45,' he famously trumpeted. 'Isn't it better to triumph by the strength of your muscles than by the artifice of a derailleur?' His uncompromising stance condemned the riders to such punishing labours that in 1924, journalist Albert Londres dubbed them *les forçats de la route* – the convicts of the road.

BE MINDFUL OF YOUR GEARS

Happily, we're not bound by Desgrange's strictures, and for the vast majority of us, gears simply make sense. But we must always be aware of what they're actually for. They're not there to make cycling easier per se (although they undoubtedly can). Gears are designed to make our human engine as efficient a source of power as possible. They achieve this by allowing us to sustain the optimum pedalling speed (or cadence), regardless of gradient or terrain.

Racers have lots of gears, closely spaced, so they can adjust their cadence precisely, conserving energy and maximizing output. That kind of detail matters when you're riding immense distances at high speed for money, and when a 200-kilometre race can be decided in the final 100-metre sprint, and won or lost by the width of a tyre. For we mere mortals, though, such a bewildering multiplicity can actually be a distraction. I love the simplicity of the three-speed Sturmey-Archer hub gears on my vintage bike, and the mere 10 speeds I have on my mountain bike. One shifter, one chain-ring, limited options. As any artist will confirm, it is when we have to work within constraints that creativity truly thrives.

Over time, most riders find that a version of the Pareto principle applies, and that 80 per cent of their riding is accounted for by 20 per cent of their available gears. So as you ride today, tune in to how many of your gears you actually use. It probably won't be all of them – and may not be as many as you thought.

LESS IS MORE

When we ride with awareness, we effectively create our own gears. Modern indexed gear systems make shifting so easy it can become a reflex action. But instead of automatically changing down at the slightest rise, simply applying a little more pressure with the legs first is often enough. If it isn't, *then* shift. Similarly, once the gradient slackens, just pedalling faster is often more efficient, and easier, than immediately changing up. If your legs can sustain the required cadence, you're in the right gear. It doesn't matter what number it is. When we're fully aware of the road, legs, heart and lungs, we ride more smoothly, powerfully and efficiently than the rider who relies on gears alone.

We're constantly exhorted to push ourselves, told that working hard – or at least, appearing to – is a virtue in itself, regardless of whether it's truly productive. As a result, we can often find ourselves, metaphorically, straining to turn gears that are much too high, or spinning madly in gears that are far too low. Either way, we expend unnecessary effort and, ironically, end up going slower. The bike provides direct, tangible lessons in the relationship between input and output. It teaches us to be aware of when we're overworking or cruising comfortably, when all we need to do is apply a little more effort, and when it's time to make a shift. Gears also remind us that simply having more doesn't necessarily make things easier. As with so much in life, it ain't what you've got, but how you use it.

The Cyclist as
Passenger and Engine

The Olympic cyclist John Howard once said that 'the bicycle is a curious vehicle: its passenger is its engine'. His observation is now one of the sport's most famous aphorisms, and for the mindful cyclist, it goes to the very heart of our relationship with the machine.

To paraphrase the dictionary definition, a passenger is someone who rides in (or on) a conveyance or vehicle that is driven or powered by someone (or something) else. On that basis, you could argue that as cyclists, we're not really passengers at all. We're not, and can't be, passive. We can't simply sit idly in the saddle while the bike takes us where we want to go, since the bike can't steer itself, and produces no power of its own. Even an electric bike requires a human hand to start and stop it. The only time we can realistically call ourselves passengers is when we're going downhill, but even then, it's gravity, not the machine, that provides the motivating force.

DO THE LOCOMOTION

Strictly speaking, we're not passengers when we're behind the wheel of a car, either. The crucial difference between the motorist and the cyclist is, of course, that the former is merely controlling and applying power produced by the engine. As cyclists, we have to produce the power ourselves; we must be the engine.

The word 'engine' comes to us, via Middle English and Old French, from the Latin *ingenium* meaning 'talent' or 'device' – as in our other modern word, ingenious. Racers still make this linguistic connection. In their world, a rider's 'talent' relates to strength, power and endurance, rather than technique (which is, after all, essentially the same for everyone, including us mere mortals). By the same token, they'll talk of a strong rider as having 'a big engine': they'll also refer to one capable of sitting at the front and hauling the bunch along in their slipstream as 'a locomotive'.

A UNIQUE RELATIONSHIP

But as cyclists, are we really engines? The human body technically qualifies on the basis that it converts energy (the potential energy stored in food) into work, such as moving and lifting. However, up to 75 per cent of the calories we take in are required by basic metabolic processes, which are essential to keep our system running even when we're at rest. To convert food energy into kinetic energy – the energy of movement – we need machines. And in our entire span of history, we've never come up with a better one than the bicycle. As the French writer Paul Fournel puts it in *Need for the Bike*: 'The bike is a brilliant device that permits a seated person by the force of just his or her own muscles to go twice as far and twice as fast as a person on foot. Thanks to the bike, there is a faster man.'

In this respect, then, the divide between ourselves and the bike becomes blurred. We provide the basic power, but it's the bike that converts it into motion. Together, we comprise a single, biomechanical entity, in a partnership based on interdependence and mutual benefit. Without our power, the bike simply stands still (or falls over). Without the bike, we're limited to the speed and range imposed by our own limbs, genes and metabolism.

HALF MAN, HALF BIKE

The Irish novelist Flann O'Brien took this symbiotic relationship to its logical (or, rather, surreal) conclusion in *The Third Policeman*, where 'people who spend most of their natural lives riding iron bicycles over the rocky roadsteads…get their personalities mixed up with the personalities of their bicycle as a result of the interchanging of the atoms of each of them'. Author and cycling journalist William Fotheringham picked up on the same theme when he gave his biography of Eddy Merckx the title *Half Man, Half Bike*. (Merckx's devotion to his craft was so all-consuming that his wife, Claudine, once joked that her husband had been 'inoculated with a bicycle spoke'.)

For the mindful cyclist, the unique, intimate relationship we have with the bike is something to be conscious of, cherished and nurtured. As Fournel says: 'When you get on a bike, it's not to forget a machine but, on the contrary, to connect with it.' Riding mindfully, we can marvel at this simple contrivance that enables us to travel across town or around the world with no fuel but food and water, and rewards our labours with liberty and speed. It enlarges, emboldens, enables us to do the impossible. It makes us, in a word, superhuman.

Mindful
Preparations

Getting ready for a ride is its own meditation. It has ritual moves – putting on cycling shoes and gloves, adjusting eyewear and headgear, stowing things in bags and jersey pockets – that switch us unconsciously from civilian to cyclist. It's a shift of mental gears, a transition from one energy state to another: from the potential to the kinetic. Call it a mantra, or simply running through a mental checklist to make sure you've got all you need, the effect is the same. Those few minutes of preparation form a cordon sanitaire around the ride, protecting its purity from contamination by the outside world. On a more pragmatic level, it's a chance to adjust anything that's rubbing, scratching, twisted or pinching, and it reduces the likelihood of getting half a mile down the road and having to come back for a pump, phone or other crucial item you've forgotten.

Checking the bike is an important part of this meditation, too. Like us, it's about to undergo a transformation, from inanimate object to one half of a biomechanical entity; unlike us, it can't devise its own mantra, so we have to supply one, in the form of looking over tyres, chain, brakes and other critical systems. Apart from the practical and safety considerations, performing some basic pre-flight checks reconnects us physically and spiritually, elevating the bike from passive, servile machine to equal partner in the coming enterprise.

OPENNESS TO POSITIVE EXPERIENCES

So what does the mindful cyclist take on a ride? When I first started cycling, I knew literally nothing, so for the first couple of years that was what I carried, not even a pump – and never suffered a single problem. Make of that what you will. I soon wised up, but then, mortified at my former insouciance, I overcompensated by toting enough tools and spares with me to reactivate a grounded 747.

Now, sage and seasoned, I feel I've struck a reasonable balance. Each bike has its own pump attached to its frame, and tyre levers, adhesive patches, a spare inner tube and spanners and hex keys in the appropriate sizes stowed in a seat-pack. When the weather is uncertain, I'll have a packable gilet or waterproof jacket stuffed in my jersey pocket. If I'm going long, I'll take water bottles and cereal bars; nothing for rides under two hours. And that's it.

Carrying a few basics is about being responsible, present and open to positive experiences. Even if you don't know how to use these things yourself, chances are another rider who does will come along at just the right moment. Over the years, I've lent pumps, tools, extra hands and elbow grease, donated inner tubes, energy bars and time, and received similar beneficence in return. Happily for us all, the golden rule of 'do as you would be done by' is still largely respected on the road.

WHAT IS ESSENTIAL?

But the question of what to take and what to leave behind goes beyond the purely practical. Most of us who ride a bike for pleasure do so for the unique sense of freedom it brings. That sense is magnified when we strip everything back, and go out into the world carrying with us only what is truly essential, and no more. To encumber ourselves with extraneous baggage does more than burden the machine: it adds clutter to our already over-freighted minds. And in every sense, it weighs us down, slows us up, and holds us back.

As the years and miles pass, so our definition of 'essential' changes. The one thing I did remember to take with me as a novice was a few coins for a payphone. Today, I carry a mobile phone because it seems silly and contrary not to (and in contemporary rural England, telephone booths are about as common as unicorns). At the same time, I see no necessity to have it switched on. I've also learned the hard way that basic eye protection isn't a luxury or an affectation.

DIVESTING OURSELVES OF STUFF

Paradoxically, perhaps, touring cyclists provide excellent models for economy and forethought. Though freighted with panniers front and rear, they carry not a gram more than they absolutely have to. Stories abound of long-distance riders sawing handles off toothbrushes, drilling holes in cutlery, and painfully writing diaries with pencils an inch long. Straws, camels' backs and all that.

To consciously divest ourselves of stuff seems counterintuitive in today's society. We feel vulnerable, half-dressed, irresponsible, if we go anywhere or do anything without preparing for every eventuality. But there's also something deliciously liberating, even subversive, about it. Like freedom, unpredictability is a fundamental part of cycling's essence and appeal. Mindfulness means being reasonably prepared, while accepting there are still some things there isn't an app for. And long may that continue.

Getting
Lost

Having ridden my local lanes daily for almost two decades, I can safely say I know my way around. In fact, you could drop me blindfold pretty much anywhere within a 30-mile radius of home and, when you uncovered my eyes, I could tell you immediately where I was, and how to get back again. Such intimate acquaintance with the country helps me avoid the busiest roads, trickiest junctions and crossings, worst traffic snarls and most intimidating hills. This is pleasant and comfortable and has much to commend it, and I can honestly say I never get bored. Yet I also have to be wary. It is but a short step from comfort to complacency, familiarity to fear of the unknown.

Hence one of life's simple treats is to take the bike somewhere new – preferably in France, which is my cycling heaven-on-Earth – and get lost.

A RELATIVE TERM

Of course, in this context, 'lost' is a relative term. When riding on roads, one is unlikely to be genuinely so; a few minutes' riding in more or less any direction will produce a signpost, settlement or friendly local who can set you back on the right route. So to be mindful is to accept the situation for what it truly is, which is that one is simply somewhere unknown, unfamiliar or unintended. It is neither a failure, nor some great cosmic conspiracy: a straightforward navigational error, a moment's inattention or a wilfully misleading road sign is all it takes. As any mindful gardener will attest, a weed is merely a flower in the wrong place. So the cyclist who appears or thinks themselves lost is in fact an explorer. And to be an explorer is, essentially, to set off with the deliberate intention of getting lost; to see and learn for oneself whether here, in truth, be dragons. If you're not stepping off the edge of the map, you're merely following others, and that is not true discovery.

The lure of terra incognita is among our most ancient and potent instincts, yet we've dulled it with our sat navs and handheld GPS. Going the wrong way on a bike ride is a low-risk adventure, a respectful nod to our wandering ancestors, and a small rebellion against technologies that, when we arrive in a new place, make us feel we've already been there.

PARTNERS IN A ROAD MOVIE

Getting lost also deepens our appreciation of and affection for the bike. It didn't get us into this fix; we did. More importantly, it's the only way we're going to get out of it. We have to be partners, the lead characters in our own road movie, where we find out exactly what kind of stuff we're made of.

Once we've extricated ourselves, there is more than just relief. There is the same deep satisfaction, the same upwelling of self-belief and respect, that we can get from fixing a puncture on the roadside. It comes from being thrown on our own resources and not found wanting. Anyone can find themselves in a tricky situation: growth lies in how we respond to and resolve it. (For my fellow men in particular, it can thus also be a powerful exercise in humility, if we're left with no alternative but to ask directions…)

THE JOY OF SERENDIPITY

The process of disentangling ourselves, when undertaken mindfully, leaves us open to new discoveries and serendipities. A missed turn can force us to make a hitherto unknown connection between familiar points, and open up a new route that may be ridden with joyful intent in future. Even the simple loss-cutting expedient of turning around and retracing our steps shows us new things, since the road looks entirely different when viewed from the opposite direction. By being present, seeing where we are and not where we thought we should be, we redraw portions of our mental map, filling in blanks and joining up dots. To extend our physical boundaries, even if unwittingly, is to enlarge our inner world.

It is good, and important, to become disorientated and disconnected in an age that compels us to be certain – and inform everybody else – where we are and what we're doing every moment of the day. The corollary of not knowing your exact whereabouts is that no one else does, either. For some, this can be worrying. But seen mindfully, it is truly liberating. Sometimes, getting lost is the only way to find ourselves again. Because at that moment, we are all we have.

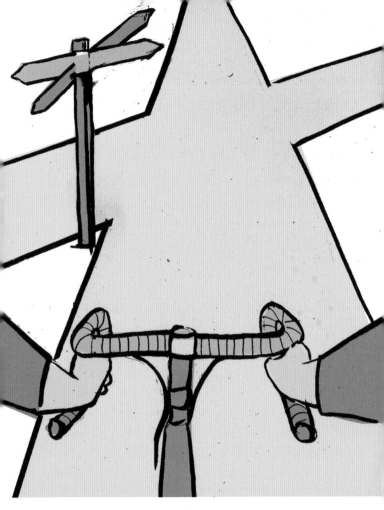

Riding without
Technology

To measure things is a profound human instinct. Whether it's distance or duration, weight or wealth, height or happiness, talent or time, we can't help recording, comparing and analysing everything around us. From this blizzard of statistics – some trivial, some transformative – we assemble a picture of the world and an understanding of our place in it, both literally and metaphorically.

This urge to know begins in infancy and lasts all our lives. Like many kids, I had a simple mechanical odometer, like the ones cars used to have, on my bicycle fork. A metal peg attached to one spoke flicked a cog each time it passed, advancing the numbered rotors inside. Even when it worked, it wasn't accurate; and when one day the bracket bent so every spoke struck the cog, it was suddenly 37 noisy, hilarious miles to my friend's house in the next street.

Twenty years later, my friends and I all had wireless LCD bike computers that calculated trip and total distances, current, average and maximum speeds, cadence and elapsed time. Then we started using heart-rate monitors too, with sensors strapped to our chests sending data to chunky watches on our wrists. Whenever we stopped at a road junction, a chorus of electronic bleeping and twittering broke out as our various devices switched to standby mode. Another decade on and it's GPS units, smartphones, headcams and power meters providing the soundtrack.

IN PURSUIT OF A NEW HIGH SCORE

All this technology is not, in itself, a bad thing. If you're preparing for an event, it's only sensible to track your progress – and all but essential if you're racing. Used judiciously, these devices can add to our enjoyment, by giving us the information we're hardwired to gather, in all the detail we could wish for. That millions of people choose to use GPS-linked apps to track their performance and compare it with others' stats worldwide tells its own tale.

But if we're not careful, we can become fixated on these gadgets and their endless flow of data. If we're looking at a screen, we're less aware of our surroundings, instincts and selves. We rely on facts, not feel; we're literally riding by numbers. (Incidentally, I trust that the follies of listening to a music player while cycling are sufficiently self-evident to make further discussion unnecessary.) At worst, we risk turning our cycling into a real-life videogame, in which we're merely characters in endless pursuit of a new high score.

As many of us are finding with computers, smartphones and other technology, the demarcation between who's in charge of whom can become blurred. Over time, my bike computer morphed from passive recorder into punitive taskmaster. I could see at a glance if my pace was slackening, my cadence slowing or the mileage falling short of the daily target. The heart-rate monitor, too, became a stern, implacable overseer, as I focused all my attention and efforts on keeping my pulse within the strict parameters it imposed. Their numbers didn't lie, and left me nowhere to hide. A poor set of figures and I'd not only let myself down, I'd let them down, too. I'm only grateful I saw the light before GPS and power meters became commonplace (not that I could have afforded them anyway).

JUST YOU AND THE BIKE

Today when I ride, I don't even wear a watch. But all those years of careful calculations left their mark. When we got back from a ride, my cycling buddy used to ask me how far I thought we'd been. It was a long-running joke that, without consulting a computer, I'd usually know to within a quarter of a mile. If he tried me now, I'd be guessing, and almost certainly wrong.

This, to me, represents tangible progress towards a more mindful approach. Because while I'm hazy on the distance, I can remember precisely where I went, what I saw, how the bike performed and how I felt pretty much all the way round. I also know when I've done enough, and when I've got a few more miles left in the tank, but it's my legs, heart and brain that tell me, not a piece of hardware.

Gadgets can have a useful, legitimate place in our cycling life, and satisfy a deep human need. But today, try going without the GPS, leave the computer behind, forget about your King of the Mountains points on Strava. Make it about just you and the bike. See if you notice, feel and remember any more about the ride – or enjoy it any less.

Light Enough,
Fast Enough

I have owned numerous bikes in my 20-plus years of cycling. Beginning with ancient second-hand 10-speeds, I progressed through unlovely steel hybrids and aluminium road bikes to carbon-fibre and titanium exotica worth more than my car.

In my desire to go further and faster – not, in themselves, bad things – I became fixated on finding the perfect machine, and the bike industry was only too happy to indulge me. In accordance with their orthodoxy, each bike I acquired was lighter, stiffer, more technically advanced and more uncompromising in its pursuit of speed than its predecessor. It was only after 10 years, too many bikes and far too much money that

I realized I was caught up in cycling's own insidious arms race (or should that be legs race?) and that, to quote cult 1980s movie *War Games*, 'the only winning move is not to play'.

LOVE THE BIKE YOU'RE WITH

The French writer Paul Fournel says: 'The desire to have a beautiful bike is shared by everyone. Some cultivate it, others repress it, but it's always there.' Mindfulness is recognizing when this natural, innocent and entirely wholesome desire is in danger of being subverted. Then, the bike is no longer a means but becomes an end in itself, and cycling quickly loses much of its simple joy.

I have learned, the hard way, that mindfulness means riding the bike you're riding, with all its imperfections – unless, of course, they're potentially dangerous or causing you actual physical discomfort. It means letting go of the mythical perfect bicycle in our heads that will magically transform us from *lanterne rouge* to *maillot jaune* overnight. According to Robert M. Pirsig: 'The test of the machine is the satisfaction it gives you. If it produces tranquility, it's right. If it disturbs you it's wrong until either the machine or your mind is changed.'

In any case, trying to buy our way to greater speed is ultimately doomed, since we ourselves are the engine. However sophisticated the machine, sooner or later we will always come up against our own physical limitations. You can have what is, on paper, the best bike in the world, but where it matters – on the road – it's only as good as you are. The one sure way to get faster, and/or make cycling easier, is to get as fit and strong as time, motivation and genetics permit. As the greatest racer of all time, Eddy Merckx, succinctly advised: 'Don't buy upgrades: ride up grades.'

A GOOD BIKE

Today, my fleet comprises a vintage bike based on a design from the 1930s and a mountain bike with no suspension and only 10 gears. They're heavy, old-school and possess not a single strand of carbon fibre between them. In terms of their technology, performance and 'seriousness', they belong in another age.

But to me, each meets, in its own way, the essential criteria for being A Good Bike. They run exactly as I want them to, and they make me happy when I look at them. Their little dings and scuffs aren't flaws or wounds but battle honours and (sometimes painful) reminders – the ink stains on the writer's fingers, the names carved into an old school desk. I know my bikes so intimately I'd instantly notice an unfamiliar sound from the transmission, or if the saddle height were altered by a fraction of an inch, or that the brakes no longer bit at precisely the right point, or that the tyre pressures were down by 10 psi.

So today, take a fresh look at your bicycle. See it not as a static object but a living thing: a repository of experiences and memories, and a true extension of yourself. A bike like this cannot be bought: it's made – transformed from shop-floor-shiny to its present state by the road, necessity, communion and time. It's so one and only, so completely yours, you'd know it at a hundred paces. Someone could build another, using identical components down to the smallest bolt, and it just wouldn't be the same.

We all have our own idea of what makes a good bike. You may define it as the latest, lightest and fastest, made from moon dust, spider silk and starlight. Or it could be the budget gas-pipe clunker that fell out of the ugly tree and hit every branch on the way down, but has never failed you yet. In the end, a good bike is the bike you're glad you took today, and want to ride again tomorrow. And chances are that, whatever the marketing people try to tell you, you've already got one.

Riding in the **Heat...**
and the **Cold**

Like the rain, the cold is often regarded as an enemy,
a malevolent force to be feared and conquered, wrapped
up against, shut out and kept at bay wherever possible.
Consider how we use 'cold' as an adjective in our idioms.
It's almost always negative or pejorative: we give
someone we dislike the cold shoulder or leave them
out in the cold; at best they can expect a cold greeting
(or frosty reception); at worst we might murder them
in cold blood. We pour cold water on ideas, offer cold
comfort, and lament others' cold-heartedness. No wonder
we balk at cycling in it.

But, as with venturing forth in the rain, there's a
kind of steely joy in braving that which others shy from,

or assume is beyond their capacity to endure. The hard man's hard man, Sean Kelly, once said: 'You can never tell how cold it is from looking out a kitchen window. You have to dress up, get out training and when you come back, you then know how cold it is.'

TOUGHER THAN WE THINK

Even if you can't muster Kelly's fearsome brand of resolute indifference, riding in the cold can be highly invigorating, given the right preparation and attitude. Tempting as it is to put on the warmest clothes you can still move in, we must be aware of the difference between standing around or even walking in the cold, and riding a bike in it. If you set off feeling toasty, chances are that after 10 minutes you'll be perspiring profusely. Much better to start out feeling slightly underdressed, and let the bike warm you up.

It's the extremities that suffer most, so that's where our focus tends naturally to fall. But since even the best gloves and socks are of limited aid, we must consciously shift that attention elsewhere. Think about how your body's core – that is, from neck to waist – is doing. This is where all the vital organs are, so we must be attentive to draughts and cold spots. (Your arms and legs generate their own heat through the working of your muscles and can take care of themselves.) As long as your core is warm and reasonably comfortable, all is well. Now consider your hands. Again, provided they're not so cold and stiff you can't operate the brakes safely, there's no need for concern.

THE MARK OF THE TRUE CYCLIST

The cold reconnects us with the world our forebears knew, and restores some of the resilience and self-reliance that our warm houses, heated cars and insulated clothing take away.

And as it hardens us, so the heat reforges and tempers us.

On a hot day, our instinct is to seek shade, stay cool. On the bike, there's nowhere to hide. It's another grounding, reconnecting experience – this time, with our ancestors who longed for the sun that ripened their crops, then toiled in its heat to bring the harvest in. To ride for hours on broiling tarmac is to labour indeed. And on such a day, the long flight downhill, or the sudden darkness of a line of trees, is like plunging into clear, cool water. Luxuriate in it, let it wash over you. It is a blessing unknown to those who now just sit in a chair, or choose to stay indoors.

Feel the heat on your skin. See how your wrists glisten, and how the sun gives special attention to your upper forearm and above your knees. Then, back at home, roll up your sleeves and take pride in the kind of tan everyone else spends all summer trying to avoid. Tan-lines are the indelible mark of the true cyclist, the uniform we can never take off.

WE'RE GROWN-UPS NOW

From childhood, we're told both to 'wrap up warm' and 'stay out of the sun'. Deliberately doing neither is a great way to tell our inner parent we're grown-ups now, and can make our own choices. And when so much of modern life is dedicated to eliminating discomfort, it also reminds us just how physically resilient we are. I've ridden at -8°C (17°F) in winter and at 37°C (100°F) in summer, and apparently survived both. It is temperament, not temperature, that is ultimately important on the bike. Acknowledge the cold and heat, respect and accept them, but do not fear them. They are transient – literally here today, gone tomorrow. In summer, you'll forget you were ever cold; come winter, you'll wonder if you'll ever be warm again. So they will pass. And you can take them both.

As Easy as
Riding a Bike?

We all begin our cycling lives in the same way: with a miracle. Even if we no longer remember it, we all had that moment where the training wheels were removed, the adult hand came off the back of the saddle, and we were suddenly, gloriously, free. The falls and frustrations, tedium and tantrums were left in the dust, the voice inside that told us we'd never do it abruptly and permanently silenced. For many of us, learning to ride a bike is one of the first great triumphs of our lives – and, proverbially, one of the few things we never forget how to do.

Having mastered the basic technique, all things become possible. We can bowl along on the flat, climb hills and mountains, and descend at speeds that set our eyes and (though not in my case) hair streaming in the wind. We can pop to the shops or roll around the globe, ride to compete, commute or contemplate, surround ourselves with company or head out alone. And all the while we can talk, sing, gaze at the scenery, meditate, compose music and poetry, eat, drink, solve problems, meet people and be at one with the world. No wonder the bicycle has been hailed as the greatest invention of the last two hundred years.

AN ORDINARY, EVERYDAY MIRACLE

But we rarely stop to consider just what an extraordinary skill we've acquired, or how casually we use 'riding a bike' as a simile for anything simple. Which it is, until you try explaining it to someone who's never tried it (or even to yourself) or watch a child trying to learn. We've all seen it: the wobbling start, the front wheel suddenly veering off course, the wild over-corrections, and the inevitable tumble and tears. Now ask yourself: when did I last fall off my bike while riding along (as opposed to a crash)? It almost never happens. In more than 20 years, I've had just two 'offs', both caused by black ice.

When, aged 40, I learned I had osteoarthritis in my knee, I found myself consciously thinking, for the first time since early childhood, about the physical act of riding a bike. I had to tune in to the mechanics of pedalling: the angles formed by my knees, hips and ankles through each stroke; the exact position of my foot on the pedal; the antagonistic interplay of my quads and hamstrings. Focusing on this repetitive, seemingly simple yet highly intricate action became a form of meditation – and set me on the path to becoming a mindful cyclist.

LIFE IS NON-LINEAR

We all know that riding a bike depends on balance. But since it's impossible to sit perfectly still, or apply precisely the same amount of power with both legs throughout the pedal stroke, the bike is fundamentally out of balance the moment we climb aboard. And that's before you add the influence of the wind, irregularities in the road surface, wheels slightly out of true, and so on. Next time you find a puddle on a dry road, ride through it, then hold the straightest line you possibly can. Look back at your trail, and you'll see not one tyre print, but two, braided together like a length of fine rope.

Thus on the bike, as in life, the idea that we can maintain a smooth, uninterrupted trajectory is illusory. Those intertwining tyre tracks are visible proof of the constant, tiny adjustments we make as we weave our way forwards, compensating for the forces we exert, and that act upon us. Bike-riding reminds us that life is non-linear. Even if we arrive at our intended destination, we do so via a series of zigzags and subtle course corrections.

BE MINDFUL OF THE ROAD

Speed is important, too. Go too slowly, and we can find ourselves weaving erratically, going more side to side than forwards, as we struggle with forces barely within our control. Too fast, and the tolerances and margins for error shrink dramatically. You can lean a bike surprisingly hard to maintain speed through a corner, but go a fraction of a degree past the centre of mass and there's no recovering. And just as a tiny patch of spilled diesel is enough to reduce your tyres' grip instantly, disastrously, to zero, so we must be aware of our own limits of adhesion.

We're constantly exhorted to focus on the road ahead. To be mindful is to identify, accept and understand what's under our wheels right now. It is also to recapture the magic we knew and believed in as children. And how many things in our busy, rational lives can promise us a miracle like that?

No Ride is
Too Short

My daughter plays the violin (really rather well, as it happens), so concerts are a regular, and welcome, feature of our lives. I'm always amazed, though, at how many parents watch their offspring's entire performance through the screen of a digital camera, tablet or mobile phone. Are they really listening to them, I wonder? Are they actually 'present' at all? And does all this filming spring from a simple, understandable desire to capture a special moment, or signify something deeper: that somehow they need something they can show and share with others to make the event 'real'? As the taunting internet slang has it: POIDH – Pics Or It Didn't Happen.

This need to record and share everything has become a pervasive force in our lives. It's as though the moment itself isn't enough – which is, of course, the very opposite of mindfulness. The dreaded multitasking is another symptom: that to be doing only one thing within a given moment isn't enough, either. So is the inexorable rise of brands over products. We are not content simply to buy something: we need to buy *into* a story, experience or lifestyle to feel complete.

MERE PEOPLE ON BIKES

In cycling, this sense of insufficiency manifests itself in the plethora of multi-day charity rides and the ever-growing number and popularity of sportives – amateur, mass-start, single-day events, usually over a choice of distances from about 30 to 100 miles-plus. The *grand-père* of them all is the Étape du Tour, first held in 1993, which every July sees 15,000 masochists tackle a full Tour de France mountain stage through the Alps or Pyrenees.

Such events are popular because they turn a bike ride into an experience, giving it an identity, and thus greater validity. When you go into work on Monday and co-workers ask about your weekend, you can say you did The Dragon Ride or The Beast, and give them chapter and verse on your time, average speed and vertical feet of ascent. Sounds so much more serious and purposeful than 'I went out on my bike'. Because in the prevailing world view, that is no longer enough.

This gnawing dissatisfaction and insecurity also stokes cycling's arms race. It persuades us that our current frame, wheels, gears, shorts, shoes or whatever aren't light, exotic or shiny enough. We become convinced they're holding us back: we're not going as far, or as fast, as we could be. The marketing narrative subtly insinuates that if we're not riding the 'right' bike, wearing the 'right' kit or doing the 'right' kinds of activities, we won't be seen as 'serious'. In short, we won't be Cyclists with a capital 'C', but mere people on bikes. And that, too, suddenly seems inadequate.

EVERYTHING IS ENOUGH

But why do we feel the need to justify ourselves and our riding in this way? Has life reached a point where something as simple and innocent as a bike ride needs a name – a brand, if you like – to lend it legitimacy? Is this why 'only' riding to the shops and back, or taking a gentle 10-minute spin round the block in ordinary clothes, suddenly feels like something we should apologize for? And does it help explain why so many of us insist on referring to our routine rides as 'training'?

When I'm really busy, and especially on short winter days, I may have just 20 minutes to spare; enough to do a short but hilly local loop of about four miles. Once upon a time, I'd have hammered round, angry with myself and the world, feeling it almost wasn't worth the effort, that somehow it didn't count. In other words, it wasn't enough.

But of course, it is. If 20 minutes is all I have, I'll take it. Any ride is better than no ride. I know I'm blessed to work at home: plenty of people don't have even that much time for the bike during the week. For them, the pressure to make the most of their weekend opportunities is overwhelming – hence the sportives, which are becoming correspondingly longer and more extreme every year.

Mindfulness is about accepting the present moment, and everyone and everything in it (including ourselves) as sufficient. So whatever it consists of, your ride today will be enough. You don't need to call it anything, get dressed up, pin on a number, record every detail, set a personal best or receive a free goody bag at the end. Nor do you need to film it in order to make it real. All that matters is that you were there.

A Meditation
on Suffering

Cyclists love suffering. There's something semi-religious, almost cultish, about their pursuit of physical extremity, privation and torment. On any given Sunday morning, you'll see them toiling up the longest, steepest climbs they can find – modern-day penitents seeking mortification of the flesh on two wheels. Three-time Tour de France winner Greg LeMond was once asked if training gets easier when you're competing at the highest level. He replied, rather testily: 'It never gets easier; you just go faster.'

In our cosseted, sanitized, ever more virtual world, there is much to be said for willingly subjecting ourselves to real, violent – and, yes, painful – physical effort. One of the most popular and charismatic riders ever to grace the professional peloton, Germany's Jens Voigt, famously declared: 'When my legs hurt, I say: "Shut up legs! Do what I tell you to do!"' His mantra encapsulates a natural, human desire to face down our own limitations, dig deep and find the gold that (we hope) lies concealed within ourselves.

THE AGONY AND THE ECSTASY

Hard riding is both enriching and purifying. It reduces life to its essentials: eat, drink, breathe, sweat, survive. And though my all-out time-trial efforts and day-long epics are behind me now, I still love coming home some days, knowing I've left it all out there on the road.

Some might argue that hard riding and mindfulness are mutually exclusive. I actually find the opposite is true. When I'm just tootling along on my vintage bicycle, my mind tends to wander. I find myself replaying conversations, composing bad poems or trying to recall some random song lyric. On my road bike, however,

I have to be wholly present in the moment, which is the very definition of mindfulness. When you're tearing downhill at 40 miles an hour on tyres less than an inch wide, you really can't be thinking about anything else. Riding hard means being fully aware of your breathing, the road surface, the lactic acid building up in your legs, the evenness and cadence of your pedal strokes, and making constant tiny adjustments to your position, effort and line. It may not sound much like meditation, but 20 minutes of riding 'on the rivet' is the best way I know to focus, clear my head and reconnect with myself and the world.

SIGNS WE ARE TRULY ALIVE

It is, of course, perfectly possible, and acceptable, to ride without breaking a sweat or raising your pulse by more than a few beats per minute. But that's not really what we were designed for. The legs may burn, the lungs labour, and every nerve and fibre scream at us that this is ridiculous, unnecessary and entirely within our power to stop. Yet these are affirmative signals, telling us we're functional and truly alive. As humans, we are hardwired for exertion, genetically programmed to endure.

And the bicycle simply, gloriously, magnifies our inbuilt biological capabilities, however modest they may seem. Derailleur gears convert energy into motion with 98 per cent efficiency, compared to just 18 per cent for a typical internal combustion engine. It's been calculated that, at a steady 15 miles per hour, the bicycle returns the equivalent of over 900 miles per gallon. Given sufficient food and water, any reasonably healthy person can ride at a pace faster than they could ever run, and sustain it almost indefinitely. Even a gentle jaunt puts you several leagues ahead of those who congratulate themselves on occasionally taking the stairs instead of the lift.

IN TUNE WITH THE BODY

Yet paradoxically, it's precisely the mechanical advantage the bike confers that makes it such a potent source of physical suffering. Unlike us, the bike does not experience pain, fatigue or boredom, but will keep going literally until we drop. The bike doesn't care, the mind whispers, so why should we? Hence there is always the temptation to push that little bit harder, go that little bit further. To do so mindfully is to find that precise point of balance between what we can do, and what we just can't.

It is important to note, however, that this kind of positive suffering is not the same as actual bodily injury. The mindful cyclist is always minutely in tune with his or her body. Warning signals from back, neck, shoulders or joints should never be ignored. Cycling is hard enough, without subjecting yourself to clothes that chafe or a bike that's the wrong size. That is simply misery. And who can truly profess to love that?

It's Not About
the Bike

Although this isn't a novel, you could say the bicycle is the hero of this book. That means, of course, we now require a villain, and since our setting is the world of cycling, there's really only one man who can play the part.

I didn't want to mention Lance Armstrong, and you've probably read all you ever want to about him, and more, elsewhere. Suffice to say I spent (wasted?) several years as a true believer, and witnessed his fall from grace with a mixture of horror, sadness, *schadenfreude* and embarrassment at my own credulousness.

Yet the shadow he casts remains long, transcending the sport – and for good or ill, he had an enormous influence on my formative years as a 'serious' cyclist.

I still own the team-issue US Postal Service carbon-fibre bike I waited five years for, then rode for more than 25,000 miles. Like millions of others, I was inspired by his exploits at the Tour de France, starting with his comeback victory in 1999. That his story of triumph and redemption turned out to be less fairy tale than fabrication is a betrayal many of us may never forgive.

A HUMAN DRAMA

Still, one truth remains inviolate. It's the title of his autobiography, lauded (ironically in the light of later events) for its candour and humanity, which became both a global blockbuster and a central pillar of the Armstrong mythology. Like the man said: *It's Not About the Bike*.

In choosing that title, Armstrong laid down a marker. This is a human drama, he was saying: if you want to read a book about bike-racing, this ain't it. He wanted us to focus on his miraculous recovery from cancer, and the tough Texas upbringing that fuelled his competitive urge – to look at the man, not the machine. It was a master stroke. As well as helping to raise hundreds of millions of dollars for his eponymous foundation, it placed him on a pedestal so lofty and impregnable it would be years before we discovered It Wasn't Really About That Either.

But if it's not about the bike, then what is it about? One could ask the same question of any sport or activity. Is angling purely about catching fish? Is mountaineering just about reaching the summit? Is writing a book merely about getting the required number of words down on paper? To which the answer is: of course not.

WHAT CYCLING IS REALLY ABOUT

So in this final meditation, and in no particular order, let's consider what cycling is really about.

It is about freedom. The bike provides a means of escape from the confines of home, work, the phone and the inbox – a chance to, temporarily, drop off the radar and disappear. It is also about reconnecting with and being aware of feelings, physical sensations, and the world around us. It is about confronting and overcoming challenges, fears and limits. It is about self-reliance and independence, and also the company of others, and encounters with strangers. It is about recapturing a sense of childlike wonder, and turning back the clock to simpler, more innocent days. It is about being in nature, on her level and terms, and directly sensing the long, slow roll of the seasons. It is about a new appreciation of the laws of physics, and finding ways to bend them, even while they remain unbreakable. And that's just my list.

It is, above all, about awareness. The modern world sometimes makes this difficult, with its constant distractions, pressures, demands and expectations. The bike gives us so many other, different things to focus on. How the legs are feeling, the texture of the road, changes in temperature, an approaching vehicle, a wild creature briefly glimpsed, a new sound from the transmission, a tight bend on a steep descent – all bring us back to the immediate moment. And when we're in that present, mindful state, all else fades into the background. If, at this moment, the bike is still moving forwards, I am climbing the hill I thought was impossible. If, at this moment, I am riding along safely and in one piece, the traffic I'm afraid of has not harmed me. From this realization comes resilience.

SUFFICIENT UNTO ITSELF

For Lance, it was All About Winning – on the road, in courtrooms, financially and within personal relationships. We are constantly exhorted, by business, the media and society, to want and expect more, both from the world and from ourselves. The awareness we can cultivate on the bike can help us to detach ourselves from desire and entrenched thought patterns and view things more objectively. It's raining. It's cold. This hill is steep. I am travelling at 15 miles per hour. That's it. No value judgement, no good/bad, right/wrong. The moment is sufficient unto itself. Does it need to be about anything else?

ACKNOWLEDGEMENTS

This book exists only because of the following:

The wonderful team at Ivy Press: my editors Tom, Jenni and Jenny for their wise words, impeccable guidance, astonishing faith and gentle persuasion; and Monica for reviving a dream I thought had long expired;

Paul Fournel, who opened my eyes to the poetry in cycling, and whose wheel I have always aspired to follow;

Mike Plumstead, with whom I had the honour of sharing the longest, hardest and greatest days I've ever had on the road;

Kevin Smith, for his unfailing good humour, common sense and companionship. 'The Rain it Raineth' is for him.

Isobel and Ingrid, who are the true reasons for everything;

And of course, the bikes.